David Abercromby

Protestancy to be embraced

A new and infallible method to reduce Romanists from Popery to Protestancy

David Abercromby

Protestancy to be embraced
A new and infallible method to reduce Romanists from Popery to Protestancy

ISBN/EAN: 9783337102289

Printed in Europe, USA, Canada, Australia, Japan

Cover: Foto ©Lupo / pixelio.de

More available books at **www.hansebooks.com**

PROTESTANCY
To be Embrac'd:
OR, A
New and Infallible Method
To Reduce
ROMANISTS
FROM
POPERY
TO
Proteſtancy.

A Treatiſe of great Uſe to all
His Majeſties Subjects, and neceſſary
to prevent Error and Popery.

By *David Abercromby* D.
Lately Converted, after he had
Profeſs'd near Nineteen Years
Jeſuitiſm and Popery.

LONDON, Printed for the Author,
by *Thomas Hodgkin.* 1682.

TO THE

Right Reverend Father in God,

HENRY,

LORD BISHOP of *London*, Dean of His Majesties Chappel, and one of His most Honourable Privy Council.

My Lord,

I *Was once fully resolved to side first openly with the Protestant Church,*

and then to inform the Pub=
lick of the true motives of
my Conversion from Po-
pery to Proteſtancy; but
upon second thoughts, ad
obſtruendum os loquen-
tium iniqua, to ſtop the
mouths of ſuch as could miſ=
conſtrue my intentions, I
judg'd it neceſſary to pre=
vent the reflections of ſome,
and ſurpriſal of others.

I acknowledge my ſelf
in this Conjuncture Ac=
countable by duty to two
ſorts of perſons: 1. To the
Jeſuites my former Bre=
thren.

thren. **2.** *To the Roman Catholicks of my familiar acquaintance : I was looked upon by those as being able to serve them at home, as I had not been useless to them abroad , and by these as a zealous Defender of Po=pery. If I can but allay the first heats of both, and hin=der a sudden rise of anger and passion, I may hope by this peaceable method to conquer irresistibly their understandings, yea, if pre=occupation stand not be-twixt them and the truth,*

A 3   *strike*

ſtrike at their hearts, and change their wills.

My Thoughts, my Lord, were not long at a ſtand, under whoſe Patronage this ſhort Treatiſe ſhould face the Publick, it being chiefly intended for the Conſervation of the Proteſtant Religion, and Converſion of His Majeſties Subjects from Superſtition and Popery, I was of opinion you could claim a peculiar right to it, not only on the account of your Character and Dignity, but particularly becauſe

of

Dedicatory.

of that *Apostolick zeal you are inflam'd withall for your Flocks* spiritual Concerns and Proficiency; whereby you are powerfully moved to accept of, and defend whatever may prove instrumental to the increase of true *Virtue* and *Christian Piety.*

I confess ingenuously, your *Deep Knowledge* makes me somewhat apprehensive of your *Censure,* but your eminent *Virtue* puts me in hopes again you will easily pardon whatever you

shall.

ſhall find defective in this method, or not anſwerable to your own Accuracy. Yet I have call'd it, and hope it ſhall prove ſuch, infallible for two Reaſons. 1. Becauſe taken wholly, it amounts to a clear and forcible Demonſtration, though perhaps each Argument it contains will not prove a full Conviction to every obſtinate Romaniſt. 2. Becauſe it relies on Self-evident Principles, and overthrows the moſt material Obſtacles to the Converſion of Romaniſts,

Dedicatory.

nifts, I mean their preoccupated Opinions, and groundlefs Fancies, That Prote-
ftants are all Reprobates,
Schifmaticks, Hereticks,
and fuch as retreat from
Popery to Proteftancy, Apoftates; but however this
method prove otherwife infallible, which the event
muft determine; one thing
I may confidently afcertain,
it will fhew infallibly to Po-
fterity, with what refpect I
am,

MY LORD,
Your moft Humble
And Obedient Servant,
David Abercromby.

The most material Contents of this Book.

The Contents.

The Contents.

Proteſtancy

To be embrac'd:

OR

An Infallible Method
to reduce *Romaniſts*

From

Popery to *Proteſtancy.*

1. THis little Treatiſe will be a Subject of great amazement to all ſuch as have known my former Life and Converſation, whereof courteous and curious Reader, take this accurate, ſhort, and true account.

2. I was bred up in my greener years at *Doway*, and in a short time became so good a Proficient in the mysteries of Popery, that I enter'd the Order of Jesuits in *France* at my first instance : I lived amongst them full eighteen years and more, and I may say, without vanity, in some esteem and repute of a Scholar being judg'd after a solemn examen, capable to teach Divinity and Philosophy in the most renown'd Universities of *Europe*, which is the Jesuits way of Graduating their own men in Divinity. I taught in *France* Grammar, in *Lorrain* Mathematicks and Philosophy ; and being graduate in Physick,

ſick, I practis'd it not unhap-
pily, and intend to practiſe
it hereafter, with certain
hopes, God willing of the
ſame good ſucceſs.

3. All this while I ſtudied
more to the endowment of
the intellective faculty by humane Sciences, than to perfect my will by ſolid Vertues
and Piety: To which I
thought the School-divinity,
as taught by Romaniſts, was
not a ſmall hinderance: The
ſpeculative part thereof, being apter to beget doubts of
the truth of Chriſtianiſm,
than to clear thoſe that men
may, and do ſometimes frame
to themſelves.

4. Take for inſtance, they
call in queſtion and diſpute,

if the Incarnation of God was possible or not ; if God can lye or speak a falshood ; if it be within the reach of his Omnipotency to condemn an Innocent soul to the pains of everlasting flames; if his actual exiftency can be clearly proved, or pointed out by the light of a true demonftration, and the like: Such difputes I ever thought, *Otioforum hominum negotia*, the affairs of thofe that have no affair to bufie themfelves withal ; I judg'd them fitter to deftroy than edifie, to nourifh and fpread Errors, than to increafe Piety and difpell Ignorance.

5. I ftudied feveral years the Jefuit School-divinity, and

and I may fay in all truth, I
reap'd no other benefit thereby, fave only that in my own
conceit, and perhaps in the
opinion of fome others, I became an able Difputant, a-
bout what ? About Chyme-
ra's, beings of reafon, as they
fpeak, Impoffibilities, and
fuch like whimfical notions.

6. Yet in the midft of thefe
hot difputes we had often for
meer Punctilo's of honour,
and a vain repute of fome
fharpnefs, I felt often the Spirit of God working interi-
ourly my Converfion, by the
fecret voice of his Holy In-
fpiration, which caus'd me
often to break out in thefe or
the like words : *Quid hæc ad
æternitatem?* What avails all

this

this for my laſt end and eternal felicity.

7. As to the practical part
of the Romiſh School-divinity, relating to Caſes of Conſcience, the World knows
how far from a true and ſin-
cere Conſcience are thoſe men
commonly called Caſuiſts : I
read ſeveral of them moſt ex-
actly, but was ſtill diſpleas'd at
their far fetch'd ſubtilties, in-
vented for the avoiding of
ſin, but in reality are the true
ſources of all looſneſs and ini-
quity : Whatever crime your
Conſcience accuſeth you of,
conſult but a Romiſh Caſuiſt,
and he will inſtantly indea-
vour your repoſe by ſome by-
aſs or another tending to his
own intereſt; and the ſet-
ling

ling of your inward peace on some frivolous diſtinction, or groundleſs preciſion.

8. Such ſort of men are great Patrons of ſelf-love, and always prone to pronounce in favour of our corrupted nature againſt the light of their own Conſcience and Reaſon, and under pretence of ſhunning ſeverity, they fall into th' other extream, more dangerous, by yielding through an intereſs'd complacency to the perverſe Inclinations of ſuch as require their advice.

9. I had great intimacy with ſeveral Romaniſts perſwaded of the lawfulneſs of ſuch immoral Practices; their common by-word was, *Les*

gens

gens d'esprit ne pechent point,
that is witty men hardly ever
sin: Their reason was, because sin, for instance Adul-
tery, may be look'd on as a
double fac'd medal ; the one
side whereof represents to us
a natural act, th' other side an
injust act ; their meaning is,
if you consent to an Adulte-
ry as 'tis a natural act pre-
cisely, you shun by this preci-
sion the guilt of sin, since an
act as natural is not sinful, but
if you consent to it as 'tis an
injust act, you commit then
a sin, which witty and sharp
men, especially Casuists, I fancy will never do, knowing
how to distinguish in the
same individual act, *rationem*
actus, & rationem peccati, the
for-

formality of an act, from that
of a sinful act.

10. So the dultish sort only, either incapable of, or
not reflecting on such precisi-
ons, shall commit Adulteries,
or any other sins for want of
this prescinding faculty :
Than which no greater illusion could I ever conceive, as
to commit a sin were not
more than enough to desire
an ill thing, or what is necef-
farily tyed to an ill and un-
lawful object known to be
such.

11. These and the like
dangerous opinions which
we shall discuss in another
place, put often my thoughts
to a stand, in order to exa-
mine what truth could be in

these

these ordinary reproaches made by *Protestants* against *Romanists*, accus'd commonly by them of disconformity with the Primitive Church of Novelties, Errors, and Superstitions.

12. Being thus perplex'd in mind and as *Hercules* in *Bivio*, uncertain what way to make choice of, I came to *Scotland*, where because of some repute I had got abroad of a Scholar, I was put instantly to work by the Jesuits; against *M. Menzeis*, Doctor and Professor of Divinity in *Aberdeen*. I wrote then in a short time a Treatise of some bulk against his way of defending the *Protestant Religion*, but neither to my own satis-

tisfaction, though several others seeing things but under one light, seem'd to be perswaded by my arguments, nor to the satisfaction of most *Romanists*, who thought and said my Doctrine in some material points was not unlike, or the same with that of *Protestants*.

13. After a stay of about two years in *Scotland*, after an accurate parallel of Protestancy and Popery, and a scrupulous scrutiny of the most material grounds they both stand on, I came to *London* as to a safe Sanctuary, where I might serve God in all freedom and security.

14. The

14. The extream kindneſs of the *Londoners* to all diſtreſs'd Perſons, and their late unparallelable Charity to the Perſecuted Brethren of the *French* Nation, could not but inſpire me with high ſentiments of their Piety and Religion.

15. I muſt confeſs here ingenuouſly, that the *Engliſh* Nation, exceeded not only formerly their Neighbours in Warlike Exploits, and would yet, if times and occaſion put them to it, but were ever, and are ſtill far beyond them all in beneficency and works of Charity, the genuine Characters of Divine Faith and true Chriſtianiſm influenc'd no doubt by the exam-

ple

ple of our moſt wiſe and
moſt Gracious Soveraign,
who as he defends and con-
ſerves by all imaginable
means the *Proteſtant Religion*, ſo favours all ſuch with
his Royal Protection and
Friendſhip, that conform to
it, by renouncing their Errors and Popery.

16. I foreſee this change of
mine, how well grounded ſo-
ever, will ſtir up againſt me.
1. My former Brethren, the
Jeſuits. 2. My neareſt Relations, who are for the moſt
part, and ever were Zealous
Romaniſts: I doubt not nevertheleſs but they ſhall put a
favourable conſtruction on
what I have done; provided
1. They condemn me not,

incog-

incognitâ causâ, unheard, and
2. Suspend their censure till
after an impartial, and intire
perusal of this present Treatise, all preoccupation Mother of error laid aside.

17. They cannot say that
any other motive but that of
saving my Soul in the securest
way, caus'd me to withdraw
from them, and side with
Protestants: They know I
was in a Condition amongst
them to want for nothing,
being supplyed with necessa-
ries sufficiently; but now I
must rely on Gods Provi-
dence and my own Industry.
Yet this I am not troubled at,
since Christ has said, Search
first after the Kingdom of
Heaven, and then all other

things ye ftand in need of, fhall be added unto you: Since he can neither deceive nor be deceiv'd, may we either think or fay without Blafphemy, he will difappoint fuch as have fetled all their hopes in his infallible promifes; but to fhun Prolixity, I come to the main point I aim at, which is to give to the publick an infallible method, not written of for ought I know by any other, to reduce Romanifts to Conformity with the Reform'd Churches: By the fame means I fhall lay open to the World on what grounds I have forfaken Popery and embrac'd Proteftancy.

18. This

18. This method to be such as 'tis defign'd, fhall be 1. Plain, that every one may underftand it. 2. Peaceable, that the will may be gain'd, and by it the underftanding fweetly conquer'd. 3. Short, that it may be proportionable to the leifure of the moft bufied, and none through Prolixity loth to read it : All this I hope I fhall perform to the fatisfaction of *Proteftants* and Conviction of *Romanifts*, if I make out with the clearnefs of a Noon Sun-fhine :

1. That *Proteftants* may be faved.

2. That they may be faved more eafily, and with greater fecurity than thofe of the Romifh perfwafion.

19. The

19. The firſt of theſe Principles proved, will cauſe Romaniſts to look upon *Proteſtants* with a brotherly Love
and Charity; the ſecond
once eſtabliſh'd, will force
them ſweetly but irreſiſtably
to ſide with them, as to matters of Religion and Divine
Worſhip; ſince they are perſwaded in a buſineſs of ſuch a
weighty moment, as is that of
our Everlaſting Happineſs:
Tutius ſemper eſt eligendum,
the ſafeſt muſt ſtill be prefer-
red before what is leſs ſe-
cure.

20. This Treatiſe ſhall
contain three ſhort Articles;
in the two firſt, I ſhall prove
evidently to all Impartial
Readers, the forementioned
truths;

truths; in the last we shall
raise such inferences as flow
naturally from these two
foregoing Principles.

ARTIC.

ARTICLE I.

PRINCIPLE I.

*That Proteſtants may be
ſaved.*

SECT. I.

1. **N**Othing makes *Re-
maniſts* more a-
verſe from *Pro-
teſtants*, than this groundleſs
perſwaſion of theirs, that
Proteſtants cannot be ſaved,
this is the ſole cauſe of their
obſtinacy in Popery; the
true

true source of their immor-
tal hatred against us, and the
very root of these extream
Rigors they have practis'd a-
gainst *Protestants*, where-ever
they happen'd to be absolute
Masters : This pitiful mistake
wherein I liv'd several years,
was as a veil before my eyes,
hindering me to see the truth,
which now by the Grace of
God I see clearly.

2. Because this Principle
is of great moment for the
Conversion of *Romanists*, I
shall prove it to perswasion
in two different ways.

1. Positively, by positive
and evincing Reasons.

2. Negatively, by shew-
ing there can be no let or
hinderance of Salvation ,

to

to fuch as profeſs *Prote-ſtancy.*

3. I can imagine but two things neceſſary to Salvation, or the attaining of Eternal Felicity.

The Firſt is to live conformably to the Law of God, becauſe he is what he is, our Soveraign Lord and Maſter.

The Second is, to live conformably to the lawful Commands of ſuch men as have their Authority deriv'd from him, as the firſt Lawgiver; fuch are Kings, Magiſtrates, Princes, and all Superiors whatfoever, in their refpective degrees of Superiority, and Authority.

4. As

4. As to the firft point, what people in the World profeffeth a more fincere allegiance to God, or a more fcrupulous obfervance of his Holy Law, than the Reformed Churches do? So as of old it was faid, *Notus in judæâ Deus*, that God was known particularly to the Jews, we may fay in all truth of them; there is no where fuch a general knowledge, whether practical, or fpeculative of his Holy Law, as amongft *Proteftants*; they read it in their Churches, they interpret it in their Pulpits, they perufe it in their Families, they make it the Subject of their private Meditations, of their more ferious Converfations:

The

The Star they guide themselves by through the stormy Sea of this World is no other but Gods Infallible written Word, whereunto they conform; or which is all one for my intent, they ought by their Principles, to conform their Thoughts, Words, and all their Actions: Is it than consistent with reason, to exclude from a capacity of Eternal Felicity, such as not relying upon uncertain Traditions, regulate all their steps by the rule of God's Infallible Word? Let us lay aside our own particular fancys, and renounce our too partial and preoccupated Judgments, and we shall instantly pronounce in their fa-

vour

vour not a little difcontent, and amaz'd at our former uncharity and grofs miftakes.

5. Their Doctrine relating to our allegiance due to all Superiors, is fo wholefome and peaceable, that I can imagine none more fubfervient to the intereft of Princes; they are infinitely averfe, and with all reafon from that irrational opinion of moft *Romanift Divines*; who teach the Pope of *Rome* has power to Depofe Princes, when it pleafeth him to fancy they are Hereticks: Whether they give a direct authority to the Pope over Kings, which is no lefs than to enflave all Crown'd Heads to the Bifhop

fhop of *Rome*, or an indirect
one, only to depofe Princes
in certain Junctures,'tis clear
they take from *Cæfar* what is
Cæfar's, that independency
on all earthly power, God
has allowed him here on
Earth. Princes are accoun-
table to the King of Kings for
all their actions, and we to
them, if we forget fo far our
duty, as to refufe them due
allegiance. This Doctrine being confefs'd and profefs'd
by all true *Proteftants*, can
we either think or fay they
are Reprobates, or not in
the way to Heav'n?

6. To banifh fuch an un-
chriftian fancy far from your
thoughts, remember what is
faid in Scripture, God illu-
minates

minates all men, *illuminat omnem hominem*, for what end? For no other but that by this light they may discover the way to their last end; if all men be thus illuminated, are *Protestants* excepted? Are they not men, and most of them great examples of vertue and piety?

7. I wonder'd often to hear *Romanists* grant such as shall never hear of Christ and his Gospel, were nevertheless in a capacity to save their Souls, provided they lived conformably to the dictates of right reason: I was amaz'd I say, to hear them confess this, and so inconsequentially deny the same to *Protestants*; but what can we expect from pre-occu-

occupated *judgments*, but in juſt Cenſures, uncharitable Reflexions, and illegal Concluſions?

8. I deſire them here to conſider that no people in the World hath higher ſentiments of God, and lower of themſelves, than thoſe of the Reform'd Churches: Which are confeſſedly the beſt Diſpoſitions can be imagin'd, to render us capable of that end we were created for. They neither rely on the Mediation and Merits of Saints, nor on their own good works, they ground all their hopes of Salvation on the precious blood of Chriſt, ſhed for us upon the Altar of the Croſs, they exalt highly by all their principles, Gods

infi-

infinite goodneſs and mercy
ever acknowledging when
they have done all they can,
they are but uſeleſs Servants,
and that all their ſufficiency
floweth from that overflow-
ing Fountain of all power,
goodneſs, and mercy.

9. And if without faith
'tis impoſſible to pleaſe God,
we have all reaſon to ſay they
are moſt acceptable to his
eyes, ſince they ſhow by their
works their Faith is a ſaving
and living Faith. Who ever
hath convers'd with them
more intimately, and will
peak impartially what he
ſthinks of their Life and Converſation, ſhall eaſily aſſent
to this, and confeſs ingenuouſly they are the beſt repre-
ſenta-

sentatives of the Primitive
Christians, so real you shall
find them in their intentions,
so sincere in their words, and
upright in all their proce-
dures .

10. How than can *Roma-
nists* without the guilt of an
extream ·uncharity, impose
so pitifully upon the ignorant
sort, causing them to believe
on their bare word and authority, without the least rational inducement imaginable, that no *Protestants* are
Elects, that to be a Reprobate and a *Protestant*, is one
and the same thing? Are they
God's Counsellors? Adviseth
he·with them who is to be saved, and who not? If a rash
judgment be a sin, as un-

doub-

doubtedly 'tis, they are not innocent, when rashly and upon groundless grounds, they condemn so unmercifully their Neighbours, who are as good, if not better than themselves.

11. Believe they not all the Fundamental points, whatever is contain'd in the Creeds and Scripture ? And if acts of Divine Love have been ever thought necessary, and sufficient means to the attaining of our last end; where shall we find a greater aptitude, and better dispositions to such acts, than amongst Protestants?

12. As *Ignoti nulla cupido*, There is no Love without Knowledge: The more knowledge

ledge we have of, and the greater perfections we discover in the object we tye our hearts to, our love is ordinarily so much the more ardent. The Reformed Churches have this advantage above all others: They read the Scriptures, and command them to be read by all their Subjects; whereby they attain to a high knowledge of Gods infinite Power, Clemency, Wisdom, Mercy, and his other attributes: Their understanding thus enlightned, their will takes easily fire, and burns with a flame of true Divine Love: The Origine whereof, is no other but that not ordinary knowledge of God they attain to

C 4   by

by reading often and medita-
ting frequently his infallible
Word: Which I know cer-
tainly to be wanting amongſt
Romaniſts, becauſe of their
ſlight performance, or rather
intire neglect of ſuch a Chriſtian duty.

13. Out of theſe forego-
ing reflexions the Charitable
and Impartial Reader may
eaſily gather, they go ſtreight
on their Journey, and not one
ſtep out of the way, who
forſaking *Popery* imbrace *Pro-*
teſtancy ; and if any *Romaniſt*
doubt yet of this ſelf-evident
truth, I ſhall be at the pains
to convince him once more,
by an argument beyond the
reach either of a rational anſwer or flat denyal, it runs
hus, *ad hominem.* 14.

14. The learnedeft fort o *Romanifts* teach it lawful and fecure in Confcience to fquare our actions by the rule of a probable opinion, yea the Jefuits hold it fafe, to ftand to that opinion which is lefs fure, and participates lefs of probability than the oppofite, though in reality furer and more probable; their reafon is, becaufe a man fo doing, acts prudently, and confequently fins not.

15. But the main and material point, is to know what is underftood by a probable opinion : The Romanifts generally, and I think none can deny it, mean by a probable opinion, that which learned and pious men hold and follow:

low : For if they be pious,
godlineſs and piety will be
their ſole aim in all their practices ; if learned, they will
believe nothing without ſuf-
ficient grounds and good
reaſon ; this definition of a
probable opinion laid as a
confeſs'd Principle and im-
moveable ground-ſtone, I
build thereon this enſuing,
clear, and ſhort Diſcourſe.

16. Who-ever follows a
probable opinion, ſins not,
does neither raſhly, nor imprudently, but who holds
that *Proteſtants* may be ſaved,
follows a probable opinion,
ergo, he ſins not, he neither
does raſhly nor imprudently
in ſo doing. The ſecond
propoſition I prove, *argu-*
mento

mento ad hominem, invinci-
bly thus, that opinion is probable which is believed, and
defended by learned and pious men, that *Proteſtants*
may be faved, 'tis believ'd
and defended by learned and
pious men, *ergo* 'tis a probable opinion, and by a neceffary inference may be fol-
lowed and believ'd without
the leaſt appearance either of
ſin, raſhneſs, or impru-
dence.

17. The middle propoſi-
tion is not unlike to a ſelf-
evident principle, and on this
account can be denyed by
none as have their Wits a-
bout them, or ſo much of
common fence and under-
ſtanding as to fee through
the

the terms 'tis enounc'd in :
Dare they fay *Proteſtants*
are neither pious, nor learned ?

Auditum *admiſſi riſum tene-*
atis amici.

I am perſwaded they will be
aſham'd of ſuch a childiſh and
groundleſs anſwer: For if
they be neither pious nor
learned, they muſt then both
be wicked and ignorant, I
know no middle, this muſt
be their inference, which is fo
pitiful that the meer recital
of ſuch an extravagancy is a
full and intire refutation
thereof, *enarraſſe , refutaſſe*
eſt.

18. But

18. But fure I am, they will grant willingly their own Divines to be both pious and learned men, yet they teach, and I was taught by them, that all *Proteſtants* are not Reprobates : To underſtand this 'tis obſervable they diſtinguiſh two forts of *Proteſtants*, the one they call material, and th' other we may call for diſtinction's fake, formal. The Material *Proteſtants* are bred up in an invincible ignorance of what the *Romaniſts* think neceſſary to Salvation, as the belief of Tranſubſtantiation, of Purgatory, and the like : In an Ignorance, I ſay, invincible, becauſe living in the midſt of *Proteſtants*, they are ſuppo-
fed

fed to want all opportunity of inftruction, and fo muft rely on their Paftors authority : To thefe they· extend their charity, and grant they may be faved; they are not fo merciful to th' others, who live they fay in a vincible ignorance of Catholick truths, which they may eafily difpel and overcome, but will not through wilfulnefs and obftinacy.

19. But to fuch alfo I fhall caufe them to be favourable, and by a parity of reafon, *paritate rationis*, force them to impart, will they, nill, they a part of their Charity : Becaufe generals produce not fuch a clear knowledge as particulars do, I fhall take
this

this particular, the Tranfubftantiation, for inftance :
The belief of this myftery,
fayes the *Romanift*, is neceffary to Salvation, yet confef-
feth a Material *Proteftant*
may be faved without it, becaufe he liveth in an invincible ignorance, occafion'd by
his want of opportunity to
be inftructed : But the Formal *Proteftant* upon another
account liveth likewife in an
invincible ignorance of this
neceffity, becaufe the Rea-
fons he is convinc'd by are
ftronger in his opinion than
yours, and fo you fhalt never
influence him by your arguments to believe, acknow-
ledge, or underftand the
contrary; what then the
want

want of inſtruction or underſtanding worketh in the Material *Proteſtants*, this wit ef-
fectuates in thoſe whom for
method's ſake we have called
formal : If thoſe, I mean the
former, be guiltleſs, becauſe
hearing nothing of Tranſubſtantiation, they cannot aſſent to the exiſtency thereof,
theſe are not to be blamed,
for though they hear of ſuch
a myſtery, yet their underſtanding is conquer'd by
lights deſtructive to it, which
diſcovering to them clearly
the truth of this Negative,
there is no Tranſubſtantiation,
remove far from their in-
tellective faculty, the knowledge of this Poſitive, *there
is a Tranſubſtantiation.*

20. Iᷤ

20. I say then they are not to be blam'd, becaufe 'tis not in the power of the will to force upon our underftanding the belief of a known falfhood, or of what appears to us evidently falfe; to conclude as I have begun, *paritate rationis*, by a parity of reafon, fince the *Romanifts*, becaufe of the forefaid invincible ignorance, grant to fome *Proteftants* a capacity of being faved, unlefs they belye themfelves, they will not refufe the fame to thofe in whom we meet with a like invincible ignorance, yea more and harder to be overcome, as may appear by what I have faid.

21. I foresee the *Roma-nist* may reply, that those *Protestants* he hath no charity for, are such as resist the known truth, for instance, they are perswaded the arguments in favour of Transub-stantiation are better groun-ded than these, they oppose against it: So they shall not be saved through their own misbelief, wilfulness, and ob-stinacy in error: To which I make this short and satisfa-ctory answer, that such men are not true *Protestants* of whom only we speak, but rather abominableHypocrites professing outwardly a Do-ctrine they judge in their hearts false and erroneous. This Objection than vanish-
eth,

eth, as being *de subjecto non supponente*, grounded on a false supposition.

SECT. II.

1. I Have proved positively, and I think to perswasion, if preoccupation be laid aside, the undeniable truth of my first Principle, that *Protestants* may be saved: For the Readers intire satisfaction, I shall make out the same in a Negative way, by showing to all not willfully blind, there can be no let or hinderance to their Salvation; what-ever *Romanists* can instance as inconsistent

fiftent with their attaining to
eternal happiness, may be re-
duc'd either to Schifm or Herefie, and that either jointly
or feverally: After an impartial fcrutiny of their beft
grounds of fuch foul afperfi-
ons, I found them all to be
groundlefs, unwarrantable,
and infufficient.

2. Schifm is a feparation
from the true Church of God,
Proteftants are not feparated
from the trueChurch of God,
ergo, they are not guilty of
Schifm, they are not Schifmaticks: All generally confefs the Chriftians of the three
firft Centuries, to have been
the conftituent Members of
Chrift's true Church; from
thefe the *Proteftants* are not
separa-

separated either in beliefs
manners, or Ecclesiastical Dis-
cipline, this I could prove to
the conviction of the most
obstinate, had it not been
perform'd abundantly, and
more than once by others :
The same cannot be said of
the *Romanists*, since they
have admitted of many no-
velties never heard of in these
Primitive times, such are in
invocation of Saints, adoration of the consecrated Wafer, Image-worship, Popes
Supremacy, &c. So if they
stand to the same Fundamen-
tals with the Church in her
purest age, 'tis certain they
have added thereunto, and
are guilty of divers Super-
structures which the *Prote-*
stants

stants were never, and cannot be accus'd of: But 'tis not so much my design in this place to charge *Romanists*, as to justifie *Protestants*, and those who embrace Protestancy.

3. They will perhaps say we are Schismaticks, because separated from the Church of *Rome* : But

1. The Church of *Rome* is a particular one, and a member only of the Universal Church.

2. As it now stands, 'tis not our rule, but that undoubted of Christian Church in the Primitive times without spot or blemish.

3. This

3. This afperfion of Schifm
fmites rather themfelves ;
For thofe only we call Schifmaticks who are guilty of
divifion and breach of unity,
by doing that which is the
true caufe thereof: That the
meaneft capacities may underftand this, let them take
notice of what follows: If
my body were united or
clofely joining to yours,
would ye not be judg'd the
true caufe of our feparation,
if ye put any thing between
you and me hindring this
union? fo you are the true
Separatift, not I, becaufe you
have thruft me from you by
that middle Obftacle you
have plac'd betwixt us both,
which unlefs firft removed, I
can-

cannot unite my body to yours again.

4. This is downright our prefent cafe if well under-ftood : The *Proteftants* and *Romanifts* were once two united bodies in the pure age of the Church, in thefe happy times when Superftition had not as yet gain'd a foot of ground amongft Chriftians, they were one People, *anima una corunum*, one Soul, and one Heart : But at length the *Romanifts* fet up betwixt us and them, *murum aheneum*, an invincible obftacle, a heap of errors deftructive both to union and unity, fo if we be feparated now, who were formerly united , 'tis evidently by their fault we could

not perfevere in union with them becaufe of this middle wall that did feparate us, let them throw it down as they are oblig'd in confcience to do, and we fhall draw up together and joyn them clofe again: Since then they gave a juft occafion, yea, and are the true caufes of this feparation, they are the Separatifts and true Schifmaticks, not we.

5. As for Herefie let *Romanifts* fay what they pleafe, it can't with the leaft appearance of truth be laid to our charge : He is not guilty of that crime, who defends obftinately any opinion whatfomever, elfe all School-men

D   and

and Divines standing stifly to their own fancys in Doctrinal points, would be reckon'd Hereticks: Such be those only who deny flatly and with obstinacy Divine Truths or Articles of Faith, which cannot be impos'd upon *Protestants* without injustice, ignorance, and calumny.

6. They deny indeed General Councils to be infallible in their decisions, but their infallibility is no Article of Faith, else *Austin* was a Heretick ; asserting, *Tom. 6. l. 2. con. Donat.* " General Councils " gathered out of " all the Christian World, " are often corrected, the " former by the latter ; correction

rection of a Council un-
doubtedly fuppofeth a precedent error and a Council
to be errable, as every one
underftands that knows any
thing : On the fame account
he fpeaks after this manner to
Maximian, an *Arian* Bifhop.

"Neither ought *Anfl. con.*
"I to inftance the *Maxim. l.3.*
c. 4.
"Council of *Nice*,
"nor thou the Council of
"*Arimene*, to take advan-
"tage thereby, for neither I
"am bound by the authority
"of this nor thou of that; fet
"matter with matter, caufe
"with caufe, reafon with rea-
"fon, try the matter by the
"authority of Divine Scrip-
"tures.

D 2   7. An

7. An Article of Faith muſt either be clearly contain'd in Scripture, or according to the *Romaniſts*, declared expreſly by ſome of their General Councils: But that General Councils are infallible in their Deciſions, is neither contain'd clearly in Scriptures, let them tell us in what Part, Book, Chapter, Verſe, nor is it determin'd in any of the eighteen General Councils, they acknowledge as the rules of their Faith; none can be inſtanc'd, where this hath been decided : Upon what grounds then hold they this as a Divine Truth, which is nothing elſe but a fanciful opinion hindering them to follow *Auſtin*'s advice, to ſet matter

matter with matter, caufe with caufe, reafon with reafon, to try the matter by the authority of Divine Scriptures.

8. The general Councils are fo far from pretending to be infallible Judges of controverfial Debates, that in a fet form *De ordin.* of Prayer appoint- *Cele. con.* ed to be faid after every Council, they pray that God would fpare their ignorance, and pardon their errors: and if they curfe and anathematize fuch as reject their decifions, this argues not they arrogate to themfelves any infallibility in deciding, for the fame is the practice of Provincial and Particular Councils, who

nei-

neither pretend to be, nor
are look'd upon by the *Romanists* as infallible Judges.

9. This undeniable truth
is of greater moment than
perhaps it appears to be of
at first: For if the General
Councils be not infallible
when they decide in matters
of Faith, none of their decisions can be holden by *Romanists* as divine and reveal'd
truths, unless they be evidently conformable to God's
written Word: Wherefore
receive they not the definiti-
ons of a private man as reveal'd Oracles? the reason is,
because they know he is fallible and lyable to error: Now
the same being the condition
and fate of General Councils,
they

they muſt of neceſſity confeſs,
they impoſe no obligation
upon us to believe their deciſions as Articles of Divine
Faith: Who then rejects as
Proteſtants do Tranſubſtantiation, Invocation of Saints,
Image-worſhip, Power of
Popes to depoſe Princes,
Prayer for the dead, and all
other points we yield not to
the *Romaniſts*, deny's only
what is aſſerted by errable
Councils, and conſequently
no Articles of Divine Faith,
we are therefore notoriouſ-
ly calumniated, when on this
account we are called by
Papiſts obſtinate in error and
Hereticks.

10. But how ſayes the *Romaniſt*? ſhall we reſolve our

doubts

doubts in matters of Faith, if
we acknowledge not the de-
finitions of General Councils
as divine and infallible Oracles? You was told before by
S. *Auftin* how to behave in
this cafe : I repeat his words,
fet matter with matter, fayes
he, caufe with caufe, reafon
with reafon, try the matter
by the authority of Divine
Scriptures, never yet corrupted in material points, nor e-
ver fhall by Gods efpecial and
neceffary Providence over
his Church ; if then you
read his Infallible Word with
true humility and a fincere
defire of your own fpiritual
profit, he will open your underftanding , refolve your
fcruples, give repofe to your
conſci-

conscience, and as great insight in his Word as he knows to be convenient for your spiritual interest.

11. This method is better and securer than that of the *Romanists*; what-ever is decided by a lawful general Council, is to them an Article of Faith, a reveal'd truth, a divine Oracle, but such Councils they hold none to be, unless the Members thereof have been really baptiz'd, which they can never be certain of, because this depends on the uncertain intentions of those who Baptiz'd them : For they generally teach besides the pronunciation of the words, *I Baptize thee in the Name of the Father*, &c. The

Mini-

Minifters intention to confer
the Sacrament, is abfolutely
neceffary, fo if it be wanting,
as eafily it may, the Child is
not Baptiz'd. On the fame
account they are not certain
if their Popes be Priefts, becaufe perhaps the Bifhop who
ordain'd them, had no fuch
intention when he pronoun-
ced the fet form of ordination: Of this I fhall fay a word
again·in another place.

12. But if the general
Councils be not infallible,
what mean the Scriptures, by
afferting, The Gates of Hell
fhall not prevail againft the
Church, the Church is the
pillar and ground of truth?
To this I anfwer, There is
nothing here as is evident relating

lating to that ptetended infallible decifive faculty of
General Councils : The firft
Propofitionfignifieth only the
true Church fhall have an
exiftency and being to the
end of the World, maugre
the oppofition of Tyrants,
Perfecutors, and all her Enemies, though it may fall out
fhe be not always vifible in
any Affembly or Congre-
gation : As it happen'd to
the Primitive Church at *Je-
rufalem*, when all her Members were fcattered abroad
throughout the Regions of
Judæa and *Samaria* ;
as it happen'd when *Acts* 8. 1.
Chrift was fmitten,
and all the reft were hid, as
it happen'd in *Elias* his time,
who

who thought he was left a-
lone, not knowing where
th' other feaven thoufand
true Worfhippers of God
were; as it happen'd during
the Perfecution of the *Roman* Emperors, and lately
before the General Reforma-
tion of the Chriftian World,
yet the Gates of Hell prevail'd not againft the Church
becaufe fhe was ever exiftent,
though not vifible as now to
the World : Her Meetings
and Affemblys being of neceffity in that juncture of affairs
very fecret and unknown to
her Enemies. She is faid to
be the pillar and ground of
truth, by reafon of Gods efpecial Providence over her
Children, never fuffering
them

them all to fail and err, but
ftill ftirring up fome or feveral in oppofition to Superftition, Idolatry and Errors.

ARTIC.

ARTICLE II.

PRINCIPLE II.

That Protestants may be saved more easily, and with greater security, than Romanists.

I Hope the foregoing Discourse will be an occasion of moderation to the most severe *Romanists*, who reflecting impartially on their former mistakes, rash Judgments, and preoccupated opinions, will convert their former zeal, or rather fury against

againſt *Proteſtants*, into Brotherly Love and Charity. I
ſay more, if they will be at
the pains to conſider a moment or two, and ſeriouſly,
the Contents of this ſecond
Article ; they ſhall, I doubt
not, let go the uncertain,
take what is ſureſt, and embrace *Proteſtancy*, as the ea-
ſieſt and ſafeſt way to our
Eternal Happineſs, ſince by
the grace of God it wants
theſe lets and impediments to
be met with in the Profeſſion of Popery : To run over
ſome of them, with order
and method, we ſhall take
notice.

1. Of their Faith and
Doctrine.

2. Of

2. Of their Divine Worship and Ecclesiastical Discipline.

SECT. I.

Their Faith and Doctrine.

1. THeir Faith is so blind, that I have heard many of them say, if a General Council had defin'd white to be black, they would believe it, whereby you see they are disposed to admit of any error, if it be authoriz'd by a General Council, though the infallibility thereof be no point of their Faith, as I have proved evi-

evidently in the foregoing Article.

2. They believe Baptifm abfolutely neceffary to Salvation, and none a true and real one, if the Minifter when he pronounceth the words intends not to Baptize, which no doubt happens frequently, fince his intention may be eafily diverted to his other defigns and affairs : Let all the World judge if people thus principled can enjoy a true repofe of mind or peace of Confcience, the only foretaft we have in this life, of that to come : For how can they know affuredly, whether the Minifter or Prieft really intended to Baptize them or not, and fo they may doubt

if

if they be Chriſtians? for
ſuch they grant none is to be
accounted without true Baptiſm; and of this they can
have no certainty, becauſe
they are ſtill uncertain of the
Miniſters intention, judg'd
by them ſo neceſſary to the
validity of this Sacrament,
that if he intended only the
meer pronounciation of the
words, I Baptize thee in the
name of the Father, &c.
The Baptiſm could be no
more a true one than a bare,
frivolous, and inſignificant
Ceremony; what trouble
then and turmoil of Spirit
they muſt needs perpetually
wreſtle with, while *Proteſtants* as to this point enjoy a
perfect Tranquility, holding
Bap-

Baptifm independent on the Minifters good or ill will, malice or intention, provided he pronounce ferioufly the words, and fet form of Baptifm, which we cannot be but fure of.

3. I was once eye-witnefs to the cruel torture of Confcience, a *Romanift* fuffered upon a doubt of his Baptifm, occafion'd by this *Romifh* Doctrine: We were in the fame Ship together upon Sea, prefs'd by a furious Storm to think on what was our only concern in that conjuncture: In the mean time this Gentleman fhowing by his melancholy looks the inward diftemper of his Soul; cryes aloud, as if he had been befide

fide himſelf, *he fear'd to be damn'd*: I queſtion'd him on what grounds he ſpoke ſo raſhly; becauſe, ſaid he, I know not whether I be Baptiz'd or not; I doubt if the Prieſt had any ſuch intention when he pronounc'd the words commonly uſed in Baptiſm; I told him whatever I thought fitteſt to convince his underſtanding and quiet his Conſcience, but could not prevail, becauſe he knew the Council of *Trent* teacheth the Miniſters intention to be abſolutely neceſſary to the exiſtency of Baptiſm.

4. On the ſame grounds they may doubt if their Prieſts can abſolve, and be truly Prieſts,

Priefts, becaufe in their per-
fwafion they are no Priefts
without the intention of the
Bifhop that ordain'd them,
which perhaps he had not
when he utter'd the fet form
of Ordination. This minds
me of a Bifhop lately de-
ceas'd in *France*, who confefs'd at his laft hour he had
ordain'd many, but ever
without intention to ordain
any : I was intimately ac-
quainted with one ordain'd
by the fame Prelate, and I
am fully perfwaded if he
were advertis'd of this laft
confeffion of his, he would
fcruple to continue a moment
in the function of Prieft-
hood.

5. Who

5. Who can relish, if he hath any sentiment of true Piety, what they teach of their Purgatory and purging fires. This Doctrine flatters sinners in their imperfections, causeth them to live more loosely than otherwise they would do, to make little scruple of these sins they call venial, and never eternally punish'd : On this account they are not so apprehensive of these Everlasting Torments we should ever remember of, when we are sollicited to sin, if no higher motive can withdraw us from it : Hell I say enters not so deeply into their thoughts because they rely on this third place : And the worst of them all after an ab-
solu-

folution got from a Prieſt, hopes to go to Heaven, if not ſtreight, at leaſt a little about by Purgatory: The *Proteſtants* who believe no middle place after death, out of Heaven or Hell, walk more cautiouſly, fear more God's dreadful but juſt Judgments, certain if they dye in the Lord, they ſhall reſt from their labours, if in ſin they ſhall be liable to his wrath for ever.

6. The Scripture is the true Spiritual book we ſhould ſtill have in our hands.

Nocturnâ verſare manu verſare diurnâ.

Here we are to gather that
Spiri-

Spiritual *Manna* to nourish
not our Bodies but our Souls,
while we travel through the
Wilderness of this wild
World. These sacred Writings are capable to make us
wise unto Salvation ; search
the Scriptures saith S. *John*,
for in them ye think ye have
Eternal Life : Yet the *Romanists* deprive the people of
this Spiritual Food, forbiding them severely to read the
Holy Scriptures, as if they
were more hurtful than profitable ; hence 'tis they live
in a deep ignorance of all
true Christian Duty, in indifferency, and lukewarmness,
without relish of heavenly
things, without true devotion, which is never more stirred

red up, than when we hear
God fpeaking in the fecret of
our hearts by the Divine O-
racles of his Holy Word.

7. They caufe the People
to contemn or at leaft to
have lefs veneration for Divine Scriptures, by teaching
they contain not all things
neceffary to Salvation, they
are obfcure, theyi are imper-
fect. They feem fometimes to
queftion their Divine Original, when they ask how we
are fure they are infpir'd by
the Holy Ghoft ; as if that
were not known to fay no
more by the Air, Majefty,
and Simplicity of expreffion,
proper to God only, as we
know the Kings Letters and
Commands to his Subjects by

E   his

his Seal and proper expreſſi-
ons, none but the King uttering himſelf after that manner: So the Holy Scriptures
being as God's Patents and
Letters to us, we need not
enquire from whom they
are, let us only diſcloſe them,
and we ſhall inſtantly know
their Divine Original, *quaſi
dei ſigillo*, as by God's own
Seal and Characters proper
to him only, without having
recourſe to the pretended infallible deciſions of General
Councils, as *Romaniſts* do,
who muſt run back to the
Scriptures again to prove
theſe deciſions infallible, and
ſo, *in circuitu ambulant*, they
turn round in a circle without
advancing one ſtep. But 'tis
not

not so much my design to dis-
pute and quarrel with the
Romanists, as to go on peace-
ably and in the Spirit of Christian Charity, pointing out
as with the finger, the great
Obstacles to perfection they
meet with, by following
blindly the Maxims of Popery: I add only here their
Prayers in an unknown
Tongue unfruitful as S. *Paul*
saith, to the understanding,
is not a small let to Piety and
Devotion; what Spiritual
Consolation can the ignorant
sort reap at Mass, or as they
call it, Divine Service, by
hearing the Priest praying
they know not what ? unless
they hold against common
sence and reason, that igno-

rance

rance is the Mother of Piety
and Devotion.

8. Their Doctrine of
Tranfubftantiation, is on feveral accounts dangerous and
enfnaring.

First, It deftroys all evidence grounded on the ex-
perimental knowledge of our
fenfes, and makes void the
proof Chrift made ufe of to
his Apoftles, in aim
Luk. 24.32. to convince them
he was not a Spirit;
Handle me, fayes he, *and fee,
for a fpirit hath not Flefh and
Bones as ye fee me have,* which
can be no conviction to *Romanifts,* who both taft, handle, and fee bread in the *Eucharift;* if they will truft their
own fenfes as our Saviour in

a

a not unlike cafe defir'd his
Difciples to truft to theirs,
yet deny flatly what they fee,
taft, and handle, to be Bread,
againft their own and the experience of all men not blind
of both eyes: Our Saviour's
Proof, I fay, that he was not
a Spirit, fhall never influence
a *Papift* to Conviction, for
though the Apoftles could
both fee and handle our Saviour's Body, neverthelefs
'tis no neceffary inference by
their Doctrine of Tranfubftantiation, that Chrift's Body was there ; may they not
fay the Apoftles could touch,
handle, and fee the appearance only thereof, as they
handle, and fee the accidents
of Bread, and not really

Bread

Bread in the *Eucharist* in their
opinion of this Sacrament,
which taketh quite away the
force of Chrift's argument
grounded on the meer Te-
ftimony of our fenfes and favours, the *Marcionifts* deny-
ing he had ever a true and real body?

I fhall fay yet fomething
more furprizing, but no lefs
true.than what I have faid before. This Doctrine of Tranfubftantiation. 1. Eftablifheth
that old and odd fancy of
fome doting Philofophers,
who doubted of all things
how evident foever. 2. 'Tis
evidently deftructive to the
whole body of Chriftian Religion : In order to prove
apodictically thefe two. Pro-
pofi-

positions, I must suppose a Third one, as a self-evident Principle, and whence they both flow as from their only source, *That our Senses in the Eucharist, are deceiv'd in and about their proper object* ; which I think can be denyed by no *Romanists*, since they confess, though they see all the appearances of true Bread, that neverthelefs there is no such substance in the *Eucharist,* but the Body and Blood of Chrift, under the veils of Bread and Wine : I see nothing, I taft nothing, I touch nothing in a Confecrated Wafer, but what my senfes are fenfible of in an unconfecrated one, but faith the *Romanift*, I muft not
ftand

stand in this case to the judgment of my senses, what I see, touch, and tast, after the Consecration, is no more in reality Bread, what-ever the constant and experimental knowledge of our Senses teach us to the contrary; they will grant then I hope they are deceiv'd, and mistake their own proper object; but perhaps because they foresee the dangerous consequence of such a Concession, some will be apt to run to a School-distinction, in aim to defend with a show of reason this self-evident falshood, that our Senses in the case here handled are not deceived as to their proper Object: They may distinguish, I fancy,

fancy, two fort of Objects, a
Mediate one, and another
Immediate, the Immediate
one is, the colour, fhape,
quantity, and other accidents
or appearances of Bread, the
Mediate one is the fubftance
it felf; our Senfes, fay they,
miftake not the former, becaufe the accidents are the
fame both before and after
the Confecration, but fure I
am, they miftake the latter,
it being now by their Principles invifibly changed into
the Body of Chrift : This di-
ftinction then cannot ferve
their turn. Let them torture
their difcurfive faculty never
fo much, they fhall never be
able to prove that our Senfes
are not truly deceiv'd, re-

E 5   pref.ntprefenting to us as Bread, what really, if we believe the *Romanists*, is not Bread. I come now to the Conclufions fpringing naturally from this granted Principle: If I mind to play the *Pyrrhonian*, and doubt of every thing I have from the *Romifh* Tranfubftantiation, a ground whereon to build this extravagancy; whither-foever I direct my fight, I can afcertain you of nothing that my eye fees: I enter into a Garden, and there I behold here Lillies, and there Rofes, I fmell them, I touch them, and yet I may queftion the truth of this, and doubt if I fee any fuch thing, what if the red of the Rofes and the white of the

the Lillies be now by an Eu-
chariftick-like Miracle the
covertures of fome other fubftances that are neither Rofes
nor Lillies; fo perhaps 'tis
not a Rofe that I fmell, a
Lilly that I fee, Fire that I
feel, an Apple that I taft, a
Trumpet that I hear, but
fome other fubftances in their
fhape, and cloath'd with their
Garments : As 'tis not Bread
that I fee in the *Euchariſt*,
but another fubftance, to wit
Chrift's Body and Blood under the accidental parts of
Bread and Wine ; what do
we know but the whole viſible Mafs of this World, and
all the Objects of our Senfes
are nothing elfe but meer accidents and Superficial Re-
pre-

prefentations of things that
perhaps were and now have
no foundation in being, or
never were, but have ever
been fupplied by God's infinite power ? Thus the *Pyr-*
rhonian Triumphs upon the
fame ground whereon the
Romanift fettles that ftrange
Doctrine of Tranfubftantiation, while the whole Body of
Chriftian Religion is as it
were a flote and carried too
and fro by the wind of this
uncertain Doctrine. For if
our Senfes may miftake their
own proper object, as confeffedly the *Romanift* fayes they
do in the *Eucharift*, our Faith
is nothing elfe but fancy and
uncertainty: Comes it not
by hearing ? *Fides exau-*
ditu ?

ditu? if than one fence may be deceiv'd, why may not likewife the other? What I fee in the *Eucharift* is not Bread; though it appears to be fuch, perhaps what I hear is not the true Word of God, though it fhine with all the Characters thereof: In fine, fince our Senfes are capable of an errour relating to their proper object, an eye-witnefs now can be no witnefs at all, or at leaft no Conviction: To what purpofe then did our Saviour fhow himfelf after his Refurrection fo often, and to fo many in the day of his glorious Afcenfion? In *promptu caufa eft*, the Anfwer is at hand, to no purpofe, if our Senfes could miftake their

their proper object, and what so many eye-witnesses saw and judg'd to be Christ, could have been his meer shape and figure, as the *Marcionist* pretends, with a clear advantage over and from the *Romanists* whose Doctrine he may easily make use of in defence of his error and Heresie. To conclude, if what appears to the eyes of all men to be Bread, is no such thing, what has been sounded in the ears of all the World, from Father to Son as a truth may prove a falshood ? Our ears being no less apt to be impos'd upon than our eyes. Which looks like a mortal blow to all tradition of equal authority with Divine Scriptures,

tures, and I difcover not yet how the *Romaniſt* can ſhun it: For ſince he grants we may all, and have been from the Cradle of the Church, miſtaken in what we ſee, may not we likewiſe be deceiv'd in what we have heard from our Fathers, and they in what they have heard from their Fore-runners, *&c*. And the rather that an ear-witneſs is not ſo much to be credited as he that has ſeen: You judge by this diſcourſe, what ex-treams theſe are forc'd into, who deny on ſo ſlight grounds the greateſt and moſt ſenſible evidence, which is that of our ſenſes: But Chriſt's Word, ſayes the *Ro-maniſt*, is my ſecurity; he aſ-
ſures

fures us the Bread is chang'd into his body, I enquire no more: Who fpeaks fo forgets, or knows not what is faid elfewhere, *litera occidit*, the letter killeth, and the literal Senfe is an occafion to feveral of grofs errors and pitiful miftakes: Chrift is called a Door, a Rock, a Wine Tree, a Lyon, *&c*. We would be look'd upon as befides our felves if we affented to all this, as interpreted in the literal fence, and according to the bare found of the words: For as the literal fence of fuch and the like expreffions, involves not only obvious implicancys and manifeft abfurdities, but moreover was conftantly contradicted

dicted by the experimental
knowledge of such as were
so happy as to see Chrift, e-
ven so in our cafe, thefe words,
this is my Body, if under-
stood conformably to the
mute Letter, both reprefent
to our mind a World of illegal, abfur'd, and irrational
inferences, and are befides
contradicted through all A-
ges by the conftant experience of all feeing and feel-
ing men : Let no Man ne-
verthelefs imagine we ground
our myfteries on the Tefti-
mony of our Senfes; we only
fay nothing can be fuppos'd
as a myftery that is point
blank againft the evidence of
fence and infallible experience, which cannot be retorted

ed againſt the myſtery of the Trinity, for though we neither ſee it nor feel it, yet our Senſes ſhew nothing to us evidently deſtructive to it, and on this account this myſtery is not againſt but above the reach both of Senſe and Reaſon.

Secondly, This Doctrine inclineth the meaner capacities to idolatry, and the ſharper wits to Hypocriſie and Diſſimulation: The common People, becauſe incapable to diſtinguiſh the appearance of Bread they ſee, from the **Body** of Chriſt they ſee not, and being taught to adore him hidden thus under the veils of Bread and Wine, are apt to, and no doubt do do frequently adore the accidents they fee, which they call fometimes blafphemoufly, God, yea fay commonly, when the Wafer is lifted up by the Prieft in the midft of the Mafs, *on leve Dieu*, God is lifted, their underftanding finding no paffage through the Confecrated Wafer to Chrift's Body.

9. As for the fharper fort of *Romanifts* when they reflect;

1. On what is faid in Scripture, that the Heavens muft receive *Act.* 3. 22. Chrift until the times of reftitution of all things.

2. That

2. That a Body can no more be without its due extenſion, for example, of five or ſix foot, than water without humidity, fire without heat, a ſtone without hardneſs.

3. That the Bread cannot be miraculouſly chang'd into Chriſt's Body, becauſe all miracles are of neceſſity viſible, as is clear by all thoſe we ever heard or read of: But here the ſubſtance into which the Bread is converted, is not viſible: This viſibility nevertheleſs is neceſſary in a change really miraculous, as it appears by that of water into wine, of *Moſes* Rod into a Serpent, *&c.*

4. That

4. That 'tis inconfiftent with reafon to fay Chrift's Body is at the fame time in Heaven and Earth, yea, and in as many places as there be all the World over Confe-crated Wafers : Who-ever underftands thefe abfurdities, will never, I am confident, believe a true Tranfubftanti-ation, though he profefs o-therwife outwardly through Hypocrifie and Diffimulati-on: The Trinity, I confefs, and Hypoftatical Union, or the Incarnation, are far be-yond the reach of our reafon, yet becaufe they are not the Objects of our Senfes, we be-lieve them with lefs reluctan-cy, and more eafily upon au-thority; but that which hath

ever

ever been, and ftill is evidently repugnant to the experimental knowledge of all
our Senfes, as the Tranfubftantiation confeffedly is, can
fcarce ever be looked upon
as a truth, by fuch as make
ufe of their difcerning faculty : The *Romanifts* inftance
commonly thefe Words of
Chrift, *This is my Body*, as
the ground of this Doctrine,
which they fay, muft not be
taken in a figurative fence,
becaufe they are Chrift's laft
Will and Teftament; and no
man, neither ignorant nor
malicious expreffeth his laft
Will by Figures and Meta-
phors: But here lies their
miftake, that thefe words,
This is my Body, are a true
and

and real Teftament, or *Chrift's*
Legacy to his Apoftles : For
he fays not, I leave you my
Body, which is the ufual manner of uttering our felves in
Teftaments, but, *This is my
Body.* 'Tis no Teftament, than
as they imagine, or at leaft
not a proper one.

10. Their Doctrine relat-
ing to the mediation of the
Virgin *Mary* and other Saints,
withdraws them from ren-
dering to Chrift our only
Redeemer due Honour and
Glory: For. though there is
no other Name under Hea-
ven whereby we muft be faved but that of Chrift, yet
many of them pretend to E-
ternal Happinefs by the merits of the Saints and the Virgin

gin *Mary*, whom they joyn
ftill with *Jefus* in their Vifits
to the Sick, either crying a-
loud to them, or exhorting
the fick to pronounce *Jefus
Maria*, as if they judg'd
Chrift's merits infufficient, or
that fome other Name, than
that of Chrift our Advocate,
with the Father, could be a
propitiation for our Sins;
hence 'tis they extol fo much
their meritorious works, that
we have reafon to fay, they
ground thereon their beft
hopes of the other Life; at
leaft 'tis certain, the fimple
undifcerning fort relys more
on what they do than on
what Chrift did for them, I
mean more upon their good
works than on his infinite merits and mercys.   SECT.

SECT. II.

Their Divine Worſhip and Ec-
cleſiaſtical Diſcipline.

1. THeir manner of Di-
vine Worſhip is not
unlike that of the ancient
Heathens, and on this account
is far from the purity of the
Primitive Church : They a-
dore God in Pictures and
Images, as he was adored by
the Heathens in the Sun,
Moon, and other leſs noble
Creatures, or rather to ſpeak
in their own terms, they
worſhip thoſe Images as repreſentations of that inviſi-

F   ble

ble and Soveraign Being, we call God: Though this was severely punished in the *Israelites* worshipping the Golden Calf as a representation of God, for I cannot imagine they ador'd it as a true God, unless you suppose they were as void of reason as it was; if then this Worship of theirs be looked upon by all as Idolatry, what may we judge of that *Romish* Image Worship the very same, or at least in nothing material differing from it?

2. Images are commonly called the Books of Ignorants, but in my judgment they deserve rather to be denominated the Books of Ignorance, because they occasion

fion often miftakes and errors: As for inftance, an Old
Man reprefenting God the
Father, a Dove the Holy
Ghoft, are apt to make the
ignorant fort believe they
have indeed fome fuch fhape.
I fhall not conteft here about
this point, beeaufe it hath
been difcufs'd fo often by o-
thers: One thing only I fhall
fay, which I think is undeniable, that *Proteftants* ferve
God more in fpirit and truth
than *Romanifts* do: Becaufe
they make their Addreffes to
him immediately, without
having recourfe to Images,
or imploring the help of
Saints as Mediators: I know
they anfwer this by diftingui-
fhing a relative and Soveraign

F 2   Worfhip.

Worſhip. The former they allow to Images, the latter to God only: But

Firſt, This relative Worſhip was condemn'd and puniſh'd in the *Iſraelites*, as I have inſinuated above.

And Secondly, They adore confeſſedly the Croſs, *cultu latriæ*, with that Soveraign *cult* belonging to God only: What then can they inſtance in defence of their innocency? I muſt as . yet tell them in this place;

3. They fall ſhort of the end they aim at, in covering the inſide of their Churches with rare Pictures, and Images. of exquiſite Artifice; their aim is, as I charitably ſuppoſe, to ſtir up the people thereby

thereby to greater devotion. But we find by experience a quite contrary effect; they are diverted from Prayer, by that great variety of alluring objects they have before their eyes, you may fee them in their Churches more gazing, for the moſt part, than praying: At leaſt, certain it is, the common fort is withdrawn by fuch outward ſhows, from uniting their hearts to God by fervent Prayer: The uſe of Images then, is not fo great a help to Devotion, as the *Romaniſts* do falſly imagine.

4. Nevertheleſs their Image-worſhip, though to be rejected, is not fo intollerable as their adoration of the

Con-

Confecrated Wafer ; becaufe befides what I have faid before, it may happen, and I am of opinion very frequently, that their Priefts either want the neceffary intention, or intirely forget, or defignedly will not Confecrate the Wafer : In this cafe meer unconfecrated Bread is ador'd, and expos'd on their Altars to the publick *Cult :* Will they fay this is no inconveniency, though the People may be guiltlefs becaufe of their invincible ignorance, and ftrong imagination of *Chrift's* Body really there exiftent. The thought of this accident, which no doubt happens frequently, with-draweth feveral *Romanifts* from yielding

to

to the Wafer, that Soveraign *Cult*, due to God only.

5. There is another inconveniency, not unlike the precedent, in a fort of Worſhip ordinary amongſt *Romaniſts*: They honour the Relicks of Saints, as their Bones, Garments, and Parcels of their Bodies, they expoſe them to the publick *Cult* on their Altars, they carry them with a ceremonious pomp in their ſolemn Proceſſions: But what if theſe Relicks be of Men that arè not in Heaven? For I ſuppoſe 'tis no Article of their Faith, that whom the Pope Canonizeth, as they ſpeak, is not a Reprobate ; ſince his infallibility was never yet declar-

ed

ed by any of their eighteen
General Councils, he is not
infallible, when he declares
this man to be in Heaven, or
that Woman to be a Saint:
Perhaps then you invocate a
damn'd Soul, you kneel before the Bones of a Reprobate, you ask help from those
whom God has rejected;
than which I can imagine nothing more abfur'd: If this
were well reflected on by the
Romanifts, they would not
be fo forward in worfhip-
ping the remainder of the
dead.

6. 'Tis now full time, left
I exceed the bonds I have fet
to my felf, to fpeak one word
of their Ecclefiaftical Difci-
pline: When I confider befides,

fides, the Written Law of
God, how many and how
heavy Obligations the *Romish*
Church impofeth upon her
Subjects, I am fully convin-
ced that Popery is juftly called, and without exaggerati-
on, a meer flavery; the
Crown'd heads are lyable to
it, no lefs, yea rather more
than others: Moft of *Ro-*
manift Divines teach without any warrant, either from
Scripture or reafon; the Popes
of *Rome* have power to depofe Princes, untye their
Subjects from their fworn allegiance, to give their Do-
minions, *primo occupanti*,
to fuch as can conquer them
if they refufe to purge their
Kingdoms of opinions judg'd

F 5   by

by *Romanists* Heretical. This you may see at large in the Council of *Lateran*, held under *Innocent* the third, third Chapter.

7. The *Romish* Church enslaves so far the understanding of her Followers, as to forbid them the use of that rational faculty God has bestowed upon us, chiefly to find out by its light the true Church, and having found it to govern our selves therein by the same, to search the Scriptures, to try the Spirits if they be of God or not, lest we be carried away by the wind of all sort of Doctrine. But this is not permitted to the *Romanists*, they must pull out their eyes and say, white

white is black, if a General
Council, though never as yet
proved by them infallible,
affirm it : This occasion'd an
ancient Philofopher to call
the Chriftian Religion, the
Religion of Fools, not becaufe they believe things a-
bove the reach of Humane
Reafon ; for that is no folly,
but on this account, that
fome of them, to wit the
Romanifts, believe as 'twas
inftanc'd in the *Eucharift*, or
Lord's Supper, that which is
contradicted by the experimental knowledge of all our
Senfes.

8. 'Twas a Liberty and
Priviledge of the Primitive
Church, as S. *Paul*
witneffeth to the 1 *Cor.* 10.24,
25, 27.
Corinthians,

Corinthians, that whatsoever
is sold in the Shambles, whatever is set before us we may
eat, asking no question for
Conscience-sake, that every
Creature of God is good, and
nothing to be refused, if it be
received with Thanksgiving;
the *Roman* Church has taken
away this Priviledge, and
commands abstinence from
Meats, ordains Fasts obser-
ved most punctually by some
of them, falsely perswaded
the best part of Christian
perfection consists in such in-
discreet Rigors, not knowing that true vertue consists
mainly in an intire Victory,
we should endeavour to get
over our own Passions, our
most dangerous, because Do-
mestick

meftick Enemys: So many commanded Fafts as we fee in the *Romifh* Church, under the pain of Mortal Sin, are no doubt, an occafion of fin and difobedience to many, who think themfelves obliged in Confcience to obferve them as injunctions of their Church: Cardinal *Bellarmine* that Renown'd *Romaniſt*, was of this opinion: 'Tis reported, he was wont to fay, that if 'ere he happen'd to be Pope, he would abolifh the Obligation of the Lent Faft. No doubt becaufe he judg'd it a too heavy Yoke, and on this account more hurtful than profitable.

9. Marriage

9. Marriage in the pureſt age of the Church, was not forbidden to *Eccleſiaſticks*; faith not S. *Paul*, 1 *Timot.* 3. that a Biſhop may be the Huſband of 1 *Hebr.* 13. 4. one Wife. That Marriage is honourable in all, and the Bed undefil'd : And 1 *Timot.*4.3.6. writing to *Timothy*, that forbidding to Marry, and commanding to abſtain from Meats, is the Doctrine of the Devils: Was not the Forerunner of Chriſt, the Son of the High-Prieſt *Zacharias*, an evident mark, that our Saviour approv'd of, and honoured ſuch ſort of Marriages ? yet the *Romiſh* Church adding

ding ftill great and heavy
weights to the yoke of
Chrift, forbids expreſſly *Ec-
clefiaſticks* to Marry,
though S. *Paul* ſaith, 1 *Corinth.*
let every man, that 7. 2.
is, whether Clergy or Lay-
man, unleſs he hath the Gift
of Continency, have his own
Wife; which Gift is always
ſuppos'd when a Man or a
Woman vows Chaſtity : So
if you find by experience,
you have it not, you are
obliged not to vow, or if
you have vowed raſhly, flat-
tering your ſelf, you had this
Gift, you are no more en-
gag'd by your former vow,
becauſe none is obliged to
perform beyond what lies in
his power, and 'tis in no man's
power

power to live continently,
without a Gift of Continency, which God bestoweth on
whom he pleases, and refu-
seth it to others as he thinks
fit ; who may, and perhaps
are obliged in this case, to se-
cure themselves from Sin and
Temptation, by a lawful
Marriage: For in this conjuncture, *Melius est nubere
quam uri*, 'tis better to Marry than burn.

10. 'Tis observable, the
most of those that enter these
Orders, they call commonly
Religious, make their vows
so young and so inconsiderately, that they hardly ever
reflect on what they under-
take, several of them protest
they are forced thereunto by
their

their Parents, or upon the account of fome other humane refpects and intereft, and if afterwards they renew twice a year, as 'tis cuftomary amongft the Jefuits, their firft vows, 'tis but with their Lips and not from their Heart: They may fin, I confefs, by this diffimulation, though I am perfwaded, their Crime is none of the greateft, becaufe of the juncture and neceffity of their affairs ; but however this Sin communicates no validity to their vow, which fubfifts not in reality, without an intire liberty, freedom, and inward confent, becaufe of the heavy and infupportable Yoke it lays on their Necks; which

in

in this cafe they may fhake off at the firft opportunity, and follow that fort of Life they fhall find moft convenient for their Spiritual concerns and good of their Souls.

11. I wonder'd often upon what grounds the *Romanifts* call thefe three vows of Chaftity, Poverty, and Obedience to their Superiors, Evangelical Counfels, becaufe I had never read in the Gofpel, that Chrift exhorted ever any to tye themfelves to his fervice by folemn vows. He counfelled, I confefs, a young man to fell all he had, and give it to the Poor, but not to make a vow to do fo: Neither could I ever be perfwaded,

fwaded, nor any rational
man ever will, that 'tis a
higher degree of perfection
to vow, for inftance, Chaftity, than to live in Continency, without fuch a tye and
obligation.

12. This is neverthelefs
the Doctrine of the moft
learned *Romanifts*. And if I
remember well of their chief
Divine *Thomas Aquinas*, but
as they commonly fay in *Sor-
bon, Amicus Ariftoteles, amicus Divus Thomas, fed magis
amica veritas*, no man's authority is to be admitted of
againft the truth, which un-
doubtedly fides not with
them in this conjuncture; becaufe their affertion is intirely
grounded on this weak and
illu-

illusory reason, that he who
vows Continency, sacrificeth
to God the thing men make
most account of, that precious liberty, they think pre-
ferable to all the Riches of
the World, which he that
lives chast without such a tye
does not.

13. This I say is a meer
falshood and a flat illusion,
for though I vow, I keep intirely my former liberty.
True 'tis *I* can't break this
promise and vow made to
God if it be a real one, without committing a sin, but this
puts me in a worse condition
than *I* was in before: For
now if *I* fall, *I* commit two
Sins, one against my Vow,
and another against the vertue

tue of Continency, whereas before I vowed I could be guilty but of one. I think then the ſtate of higheſt perfection is that which removeth us fartheſt from ſin and the occaſions thereof, which certainly vows do not, but enſnaring men rather becauſe of their great weakneſs and frailty, expoſe them to both by that perverſe, though inbred inclination of theirs, to whatever is forbidden them; for nothing more true than *nitimur in vetitum ſemper,* &c.

14. This engageth me here to the defence of an Aſſertion, which will be looked upon as a Paradox by the Romaniſts, yet if reflected

on

on without preoccupation, is a clear, fimple, and undeny-able truth : They dry up all the veins of their Eloquence in extolling a Religious Life, as they call it : they fay it is moft perfect, happy, bleffed, and what not : read *Jerome Platus* on this Subject , and you fhall find him as whim-fical in his notions of this ima-ginary happinefs , as *Plato* was in his abftract Idea's.

15. I can prove to per-fwafion there is no way of ferving God more dangerous, and wherein you fhall meet with greater obftacles to your fpiritual progrefs and eternal happinefs, than in thefe pretended Religious Or-ders, as they now ftand of the

the Romiſh Church ; my reaſon is clear, and runs thus,
becauſe their yoak is incom-
parably greater and heavier
than that of other Chriſtians,
ſince beſides the Commands
of God and their Church,
they tye themſelves to a num-
berleſs number of petty ob-
ſervances and rules, which
though they confeſs bind not
their conſcience, yet they
teach none of them can ſcarce
ever be tranſgreſſ'd without
ſin, either *ratione ſcandali*, by
reaſon of the ſcandal, or *ratione contemptus*, becauſe of the
contempt of Authority, or on
ſome other account; they ſay as
yet ſomething more ſtrange,
that *non progredi, regredi eſt*,
'tis not enough for them to
observe

obferve the Commands of
God and the Church, they
call that *non progredi*, no progrefs, unlefs they do more
than he has commanded, by
ftanding with as great pre-
cifenefs to their Cuftoms and
Rules, as if they were an ef-
fential part of Gods written
Law.

15. In what fears then, if
they have a timorous confcience; in what troubles and
turmoils, and what vexation
of fpirit they live in : for if
fo few keep Gods Commands,
as 'tis faid the Juft falls feven
times a day, what judgment
may we frame of them who
pretend to do more than he
has ordain'd, by obferving a
number innumerable of petty
Rules.

Rules, Statutes, and frivolous
Cuftoms. On this account I
have heard feveral amongft
them fay what I believe to
be moft true, that their yoke
was not like to the yoke of
Chrift, fweet and light, *Jugum fuave & onus leve*, but
rather exceedingly bitter,
and moft heavy, *Jugum ama-
rum & onus grave*.

16. In fine, I may affirm,
without deviating from the
Truth, That thefe *Romifh*
Vows are rather Snares to
intrap Souls, than true means
to their attaining to a higher
degree of Glory in Heaven.
The Devil overcomes fome
by manifeft Temptations, and
a flat Propofition of Sin, but
becaufe fome others, defirous

G   to

to live after a more perfect manner, admit not so easily of his Suggestions, he catcheth them by their own inclinations, by vowed engagements, to the pursuance of a Perfection, which, through Humane Frailty, they shall never reach to ; so weary to swim always against the water, they are forc'd, at length, to yield to the stream, and go downwards, which was the Enemies sole aim and main design.

17. Out of this foregoing Discourse, we may conclude, Protestants to be most happy, as meeting with none of these forementioned Obstacles, to their eternal happiness, so long as they follow the

Maxims

Maxims of true Proteſtancy. For,

Firſt, Their Faith is not ſo blind, though ſubmiſſive enough to Church Authority, as to hold for Divine Truths, the fanciful Opinions of fallible Men, or Deciſions of errable Councils: The Word of God onely is their Rule, to this they are taught to conform their Faith and their Actions.

Secondly, They are not tortur'd and turmoil'd with Doubts, if they be Baptiz'd or not, becauſe they know the Exiſtency of Baptiſm to be independant on the Miniſters uncertain intentions.

Thirdly, They have no Incitement to Sin, by relying

on

on a middle place between
Heaven and Hell; they hold
no Purgatory, and so are
powerfully deterr'd from of-
fending God, through fear of
his terrible Justice exercis'd
in Hell, upon such as die
without Repentance.

Fourthly, They reject the
dangerous distinction of Venial, and Mortal Sin, as open-
ing a door to Loosenes; for
though some Sins be more
heinous than others, yet in
this we must confess a perfect
equality, that they are all of-
fences of an infinite Majesty,
and consequently deserve his
eternal Wrath, as being of an
unlimited malice.

Fifthly, They allow every
one to read the Scripture as
the

the Fountain of all wholefom
Doctrine , and capable to
make us wife unto Salvation,
as being a Light to our Underftanding, left we err; and
a Fire to our Will, left we
wax Cold in Charity and
Love towards God and our
Neighbors.

Sixthly, Their Doctrine
concerning the Lord's Supper is fpirit and life, it gives
no occafion either of Idolatry or Hypocrifie, by teaching that ftrange Novelty of
Tranfubftantiation: They ca-
ptivate indeed their underftanding *in obfequium Fidei,*
in obedience to Divine Faith,
but pull not out their Eyes
to believe there is no Bread
in the Eucharift, where they

G 3   fee

fee all the infeparable Proper-
ties thereof, as Colour, Shape,
Quantity, &c.

Seventhly, They rely folely
on the Merits of Chrift; neither on the mediation of
Saints, nor on their own good
works, fully perfuaded of
this Chriftian Truth, when
they have done all they can,
they are but ufelefs Servants,
and that all their fufficiency
is from Above.

Eighthly, Their Divine
Worfhip is pure, and without mixture of Superftition
or Idolatry; neither intirely
without Ceremonies, nor o-
verburden'd with 'em fuper-
ftitioufly.

Ninthly, They adore God
in Spirit and Truth, not under

der corporal Shapes, and falſe
Repreſentations; they adore
him as Spirit and Truth, as he
is in reality, knowing perfect-
ly all their ſpiritual needs, and
bodily neceſſities, without the
help of Saints as Speakers and
Informers.

Tenthly, Their Eccleſiaſti-
cal Diſcipline is moſt conformable in all its parts to that of
the Primitive Church, as alſo
their Faith, their Manners, and
way of living, as may be gathered out of this and the
foregoing Article; and every one knows that is not al-
together a Stranger to Anti-
quity.

Eleventhly, They ſerve
God in all freedom of ſpirit,
without endangering their

G 4   Souls

Souls by vows of Continency, true Snares rather to Innocency, than fit means for
attaining to Perfection and
eternal Felicity.

ARTIC.

ARTICLE III.

SECT. I.

Conclusions flowing from the first Principle of this Method.

I. MY first Principle was, That those who profess Protestancy, may be saved. I proved it to Conviction, without invectives or bitterness, in the spirit of Christian

Chari-

Charity, Meeknefs and Leni-
ty, perfuaded of this clear
Truth, that Conviction of the
intellective Faculty worketh
never a true Converfion, unlefs the Will be conquer'd by
a civil and charitable way of
debating.

II. 'Tis Proverbial amongft
the *Romanifts*, That out of
the Church there is no hopes
of falvation.   In what fenfe
this is true, 'tis not my defign
here to inquire ; but I affirm they are pitifully mifta-
ken, underftanding by the
Church, that handful of Chriftians united together in
communion with the See of
Rome, which is as unreafo-
nable,

nable, as if one would say,
a Particular is an Univerſal,
a Part is the Whole, or at
leaſt of as great and vaſt a
bulk. They will grant then,
I ſuppoſe, *Proteſtants* to be
Members of the Univerſal
Church, but dead ones, deſti-
tute of life, ſpirit and vigour.
The contradictory of this
Propoſition ſtands demon-
ſtrated in the firſt Article ;
for ſince they may be ſaved
by the merits and influence
of their inviſible Head
Chriſt, they are both whole-
ſom, living, and vigorous
Members of his Church.

III. They cannot be accu-
ſed of Schiſm, nor without a
ground-

groundless Calumny called *Schismaticks*, since they are still contain'd in the Catholick or Universal Church, their Reform being in the Church, not from it; hold they not all Points necessary to salvation, and whatever was of Divine Faith in the primitive Times. They separated, I confess, from the particular Church of *Rome*, but *Romanists* were the true causes of this Separation, by introducing Errors and Novelties, so they are properly the *Separatists*, not *Protestants*: Let them be ashamed then to sound perpetually as they do in the Peoples ears, such a notorious Calumny, which

which with greater truth
may be Retorted againſt
themſelves.

IV. I hope hereafter they
ſhall prove more moderate,
and call them Brethren,
whom they have thought hitherto Hereticks ; for I am
perſuaded they are convinc'd
this foul aſperſion of Hereſie
is groundleſs, as being a meer
illuſion, and the product of a
preoccupated judgment. The
Proteſtants, ſay they, are Hereticks, becauſe they reject
obſtinately the Deciſions of
General Councils ; but will
they never reflect that theſe
Deciſions can neither be
looked upon by us , nor by
them

them as revealed Truths, unlefs their Infallibility be either grounded on clear Scripture, or in their fentiment on the Authority of fome General Council. In what Scripture is it faid, General Councils are infallible Judges of Controverfial Debates? In what Council was it decided, that General Councils were unerrable? Here they are amaz'd, and their thoughts at a ftand; they are forced to yield, and confefs ingenuoufly, that this pretended Infallibility hath no other foundation in being, but that of their own Opinion and Fancy: For though 'twere grounded on the Decifion

of

of some General Council,
this must be first proved Infallible by an Evidence di-
stinct from its own Testi-
mony.

V. But because my onely
design in this place is to raise
Inferences, and not to frame
new Arguments, I entreat the
Romanist Reader, after a se-
rious perusal of my first Article, to reflect a moment
upon his own Uncharity a-
gainst so many Thousands of
His Majesties Subjects, and
other Nations, so commen-
dable for their unstain'd Life
and Conversation; so acceptable to God, because of their
Virtue and Innocency. Let
them,

them, I say, upon second thoughts, repent of their former Uncharity, in condemning their Neighbors so inconsiderately, as *Schismaticks*, *Hereticks*, *Reprobates*. Let them detest from the bottom of their hearts this Unchristian Rigor and Severity; if perhaps upon such groundless pretences they were persuaded 'twas lawful to persecute them by Treason, Fire and Sword, the deep ignorance they liv'd in could be as a Veil to the Enormity of their Crime: But after the perusal of this Treatise they can no more pretend ignorance, they are told of their Errour, and sufficiently ly inform'd of their former miftakes.

VI. Neither can they with the leaft appearance of Truth call *Apoftates* fuch as embrace *Proteftancy*, fince they retain ftill the Faith of that Church which flourifhed the firft three Centuries after our Saviour's Birth, and is confeffed by all Parties to have been the true Church of Chrift. They admit not indeed the additional Articles of *Purgatory,Tranfubftantiation,Imageworfhip, Invocation of Saints,* *&c.* for the grounds above laid. But on this account they are in no true fenfe *Apoftates*,becaufe *Apoftafie* is a defection

fection from the true Faith,
and these Points are either
gross Errors, or, as a learned
Divine of the *English* Church
calls them, inferiour Truths,
not destructive to Divine
Faith, whether believ'd or de-
nied ; though they be, as I
have insinuated elsewhere,
not a little prejudicial to
true Virtue, and Christian
Piety.

VII. Rashness or Impru-
dence can with as little justice
be objected to such as retreat
from *Popery*. It has been de-
monstrated by the consent
of *Romanists*, and self-evident Principles they follow,
by professing *Protestancy* a
pro-

probable and well-grounded opinion, That worſhipping God after the Proteſtant manner, they may attain to the end they were created for, which is eternal happineſs.

SECT.

SECT. 2.

Conclusions flowing naturally from the second Principle of this method.

THE second Principle was, *That Protestants may be saved more easily, and with greater security, than those of the Romish Persuasion.* I shall not repeat here what I said before, to explain, rather than to prove this self-evident Truth, hence only I infer what is evident enough of it self without any formal inference.

I. That

I. That *Romish Priests* are obliged not to endeavor, as they do, the Conversion, or rather Perversion of *Prote-stants*, because 'tis a sin to withdraw any man from the safest way to Heaven.

II. The *Romanists* once convinc'd, as I hope they are, of this second Principle, must of necessity renounce *Popery*, and profess *Protestancy*, there being an obligation incumbent to all men in matters of such a high Concern, to chuse that which is secureft.

III. *Protestants* must stand stoutly to their own Religion,

on, and way of Divine Worſhip, and cannot, if they re-
gard a good Conſcience, after
this inſtruction turn *Romaniſts*, becauſe in ſo doing they
would endanger their own
Souls, by reaſon of the forementioned obſtacles to ſalva-
tion in the profeſſion of *Popery*.

IV. All true *Proteſtants*,
and more particularly Thoſe
who by their Dignity, Of-
fice, and Imployment, are to
watch over the Flock, muſt
needs, if they will perform
their duty, endeavour with
all Charitable and Chriſtian
means the Confirmation of
Proteſtants in *Proteſtancy*,
and

and the Converſion of their Popiſh Subjects from *Popery*, elſe they forfeit their Character and Miniſtry, as neglecting the ſpiritual concerns of Souls redeem'd by the precious blood of Chriſt, and committed to their truſt and vigilancy : If I have been my ſelf inſtrumental to the perverſion of ſeveral, while miſled by a blind Zeal, I ſaw things but under one light, I ſhall, at Conveniency, repair this Damage done to the Church, by writing in my ſpare-hours ſuch inſtructions as may be ſubſervient to their returning homewards, or uſeful to the converſion of others, and particularly

cularly my neareſt and dea-
reſt Relations.

V. I ſhall put here a ſtop
to my Pen , and an end to
this Treatiſe , with a ſhort
and charitable Advice to all
His Majeſties Subjects of the
Romiſh Perſuaſion.

Chari-

Charitable Advice to all His Majesties Subjects of the Romish Persuasion.

YOu have believ'd till now, as an Article of your Faith, That Proteſtants were all Reprobates, Hereticks, Schiſmaticks, and

H   many

many of them Apo-
ſtates. Your Faith being
ever an implicite one,
and pinn'd on other
mens ſleeves. You are
more to be pitied for
this groſs miſtake , than
blam'd. You are not
unlike, pardon me the
freedom of this Parallel,
to thoſe that are blind
from their birth. You
may induce ſuch men to
believe any Falſhood
you pleaſe , as for in-
ſtance , that White is
Black, or Black is White,
be-

becaufe they want the
ufe of their vifive Fa-
culty, and folely relie on
your Authority. You re-
nounce not only to your
reafon, in favour of the
pretended Council-Ora-
cles. You hold not only
your underftanding ca-
ptive when *Rome* fpeaks,
but you extinguifh the
cleareft light thereof, in
fubmiffion to her De-
cifions, as if you were
quite blind, and under-
ftood nothing, or as if
Nature had not beftow-

H 2 ed

ed upon you an intellective Faculty, in order to difcern good from evil, falfhood from truth, to try the fpirits whence they are, whether of God or not. The *Romanifts*, your Mafters, imitate thofe ancient Heathens, who, to gain the Peoples efteem and greater veneration for their Laws, faid confidently, They had received them immediatly from the gods: So they, to hold you in awe, and tyrannize over

your

your underſtandings, as
by a principle of Con-
ſcience, call boldly whatever is decided in Gene-
ral Councils, Divine O-
racles, Reveal'd Truths,
Faith-Articles, which is
the greateſt Artifice the
Prince of Darkneſs could
invent, to ſpread all the
World over Error, Igno-
rance, and Superſtition.
To avoid then your be-
ing ſeduc'd hereafter,
make uſe of your Rea-
ſon, ſince 'tis chiefly allow'd you for your at-

tain-

taining to the know-
ledge of faving Truths,
peruse often, and me-
ditate frequently this
Treatise, wherein you
shall discover clearly,

I. That *Proteftants*,
you have been so averse
from hitherto, through
preoccupation and igno-
rance, may be saved, as
being true Members of
the Universal Church,
and neither Hereticks
nor Schismaticks.

II. That

II. That they attain to Eternal Happinefs more eafily, and with greater fafety than *Romanifts*, ftanding to the Principles of *Popery*.

III. That the boaft-ed of Infallibility of General Councils is no Article of Faith amongft *Roman=Catholicks*, but a meer politick defign to domineer by this perfua-fion over all Nations, for the increafe of tem-poral Concerns ; and that

that as *Rome* of old fub-
dued the World by force
of Arms, fhe may ftill
enflave it by Religious
Scruples, and ftrong Fan-
cies of the Divine Ori-
ginal of her Oracles ,
which was meant by the
Poet that fung thus :

*Roma caput mundi, quicquid
non poffidet armis Reli-
gione tenet.*

You have pretended
formerly your Confci-
ence fuffered you not to
con-

conform to that Divine
Worſhip now eſtabli-
ſhed by Law in theſe
three Kingdoms , you
thought it not lawful to
forſake *Popery*, and profeſs *Proteſtancy*, as being
in your opinion nothing
elſe but Hereſie, Schiſm,
Apoſtaſie. This can be
no more an Obſtacle to
your Converſion , you
are now informed to
Conviction of the con-
trary , and of your in-
cumbent Obligation to
retreat from *Romaniſm* ;
of

of two Evils, the leaſt
is to be choſen; and of
two ways to Heaven,
that which is ſecureſt, in
matters of this Concern
all deliberation laid a-
ſide, your Conſcience
will preſs you to the ſu=
reſt. So long as you en=
deavour your being in=
ſenſible to her Checks,
you pretend in vain to
any true happineſs in
this life, ſhe will ſound
perpetually in your ears
the extreme danger you
are in through your
own

own fault, and as an in-
feparable, terrifying, and
threatning Ghoſt, diſturb
your Repoſe by day
and by night, *in all times,
and in all places.*

Omnibus umbra locis aderit.

FINIS.